Howard Nemerov on *Herbert Woodward Martin and the African American Tradition in Poetry:*

Herbert Woodward Martin's combination of plainest direct assertion with gnomic and riddling question makes his voice convincing when he faces up to, as he does in the best of his poems, the themes of pain, grief, and loss. He deals with human helplessness honestly and courageously.

Other Books by Herbert Woodward Martin

Inscribing My Name: Selected Poems New, Used, and Repossessed. (Kent State University Press 2006)

Escape to the Promised Land. (Bottom Dog Press 2005).

In His Own Voice. (Ohio State University Press, 2002).

Galileo's Suns in *Dunbar Suns and Dominions,* ed. David Shevin. (Bottom Dog Press 1999).

A Rock Against the Wind. (Berkley Books, 1996).

The Forms of Silence. (Lotus Press 1980).

The Complete Novels of Paul Laurence Dunbar Editors: Herbert Woodward Martin, Ronald Primeau, and Gene Andrew Jarrett. (Ohio University Press / Swallow Press, 2010).

On the Flyleaf

Poems

Herbert Woodward Martin

Harmony Series
Bottom Dog Press
Huron, Ohio

ISBN 978-1-933964-73-74-4
Bottom Dog Publishing
PO Box 425, Huron, Ohio 44839
http://smithdocs.net
e-mail: Lsmithdog@smithdocs.net

First Edition

Credits:
General Editor: Larry Smith
Cover Design: Susanna Sharp-Schwacke
Author Photo: David Schock from the film
*Jump Back, Honey: The Poetry and Performance
of Herbert Woodward Martin*

Acknowledgments

We thank the following publications where these poems first appeared:

On the Flyleaf of *April Galleons, Foliate Oak Literary Review;*
On the Flyleaf of *The Answers Are in the Mountains, Fog Dog
Literary Review;* On the Flyleaf of *The Answers Are in the
Mountains, Kerf;* On the Flyleaf of *By the Light of My Father's
Smile, Common Sense;* On the Flyleaf of *The Book of Light, HQ
Magazine;* On the Flyleaf of *The Book of Light, FreeXpression;*
On the Flyleaf of *Collected Poems, Foliate Oak Literary Review;*
On the Flyleaf of *Cold Comfort, The Dead Mule Society;* On the
Flyleaf of *The Divided Country, Notre Dame Review;* On the
Flyleaf of *The Leaves of Hypnos, FreeXpression;* On the Flyleaf of
The Master Letters, Foliate Oak Literary Review; On the Flyleaf
of *Musical Events, House Organ;* On the Flyleaf of *The October
Palace, Kerf;* On the Flyleaf of *Plenty, FreeXpression;* On the
Flyleaf of *Selected Poems, FreeXpression;* On the Flyleaf of *The
Silent Singer, Confluence;* On the Flyleaf of *Small Congregations I,
Notre Dame Review;* On the Flyleaf of *Small Congregations II,
Plain Spoke;* On the Flyleaf of *Steal the Bacon, The Dead Mule
Society;* On the Flyleaf of *Swan's Island, The Dead Mule Society;*
On the Flyleaf of *Swan's Island, Foliate Oak Literary Review;*
On the Flyleaf of *Transformation, The Dead Mule Society;* On the
Flyleaf of *Two by Two, Mock Turtle Review.*

Contents

The flyleaf poems initially were the results of my not having my notebook with me or beside my bedside at night. The clear implication is that influences pervade our minds and our bodies whether we seek them out or not. The Muse is constantly at work dancing a dervish or a Tarentella whipping up the mind and body in unexpected ways. No poet I have ever read is to be blamed for the flaws in my poems, even if I did write something on the flyleaf of their book. As art speaks to other art these poems were prompted by poems read and conceived and written sometime later. Fathered and mothered, as it were, they have a life of their own.

For: Julia and Athena

Mary Ann,

Lyncheryl

and Lauren

for: an aunt and uncle

who disappeared

before I was born

On the Flyleaf of *The Silent Singer*

Work arrives.

He carries a gun

loaded with point blank metaphors,

demands the best young male in the class,

takes him away at gunpoint.

I am unable to restrain them with music.

There were seeds in that male

whose roots were ready to grow

into tutored gardens.

Now he has been missing for weeks.

In bars and mines,

he digs with his hands

nightly and daily,

for the personification of money,

the seduction of feminine allure.

He has not yet learned,

how to keep the wolves from eating his heart.

On the Flyleaf of *The Book of Light*

    For: Sara

In the moment of final farewell

she pressed, with her hands, down

hard on the smooth oak of his house

as if to push all of her blood magic,

her bone strength electric to revive

his still body; nothing happened.

She had to walk away that day,

down a modest hill with only

her memories of him intact.

They would last; they would last.

On the Flyleaf of *Selected Poems*

When a man dies, he doesn't have to wipe his ass anymore,

nor does he have to loosen those last drops of urine from

his penis; it is all over, except the bathing and dressing

which is left to the undertakers in North America.

Everywhere else you are quickly buried in what you have on.

Black people think of it as being "Dressed to Kill."

It means you have stepped out of a bandbox,

that Messers Gucci and Saint Laurent along with

Ms. Chanel have themselves dressed you as if you were

alive, kicking and smelling as fresh and delightfully wintry,

without their ever imagining the journey they have so

successfully prepared you for.

On the Flyleaf of *The Answers Are Inside the Mountains* I

   For: Susan Doyle

America, someone is singing in Walt Whitman's shoes

in possession of an astounding black voice which

can be heard while no one was prepared to listen

or to entertain such unique song.

Who could scale those monumental melodies

like the great Italians who uttered full-voiced

those challenging Germanic sounds, requiring

one to thunder madly at the heavens with angry

fists, afraid of being commonplace or too reticent

to declare how daring one must be to speak truth?

Whitman's footsteps have been, modestly,

preserved in silence, whatever passageways may be taken.

On the Flyleaf of *The Answers Are Inside the Mountains* II

Walt Whitman we have learned a new sound watching birds
resting on electrical wires of the cities we inhabit, they listen
with their feet to the magnificent cords of electricity flowing
magically from one place to another while admitting that some
distortion leads to accuracy if only by accident, because the
speech we employ, even as it is generated, is sometimes distorted
by those large empty spaces we refer to as pauses.

On the Flyleaf of *April Galleons*

The terror in my heart is like a Russian schoolyard.

Grief is a part of the song the Russian mothers sing.

A black mother, a continent away, says:

Our children are supposed to bury us;

what is it that forces us to lay them in the earth?

I hear the blood as it thunders in my ears;

it drowns the words of powerful men who tell us lies.

We know in our skeletons that they cannot be trusted.

I shall gather up all my black dignity

along with all of my reserve and resolve,

and strut carefully, head erect, eyes forward

looking squarely at that bier:

which contains what once was promise,

which was cheered at birth and now we mourn,

which demands we understand our faulty grief.

On the Flyleaf of *The Book of Light*

My Caucasian friends are curious to a misdemeanor.

They want to know the adoptive meaning of black.

What is this century-old mystery of survival?

What is the buoyancy that lies beneath my skin?

I say: "There is no secret formula,

no fairy Godmother appearing from out of nowhere,

no three wishes given,

no daring prince arriving with a working entourage

carrying with them a matching, naked slipper,

and no princess to be rescued."

I repeat: "Change lives in my blood."

My friends may never understand that

change is placing one tedious foot in front of another.

On the Flyleaf of *Two by Two*

Since slavery was so horrific,
I have decided to take revenge
on eternity and sit the entire
session out quietly and not do
one lick of work even for the
kindest of angels since seeing as how
my ancestors did so much work and
never earned one cent of pay, and if
by some hell of a chance I land in
eternal punishment, I will call it even
or justifiable recompense but not
revenge or payback. No use rubbing
mud in the face of whoever is in
charge, and especially since heaven
and hell are supposed to represent
goodness and peace.

On the Flyleaf of *The October Palace* II

For Christian

Five inches of new snow

has fallen on languishing

snow, beneath which, we

must finally attempt to see

and discover, as well as,

remind ourselves simply

of how much beauty is

contained in small things.

On the Flyleaf of *The Invention of The Zero*

Rain throttles through the fall trees.

Indian arrowheads sharp with attack

puncture the immediate heart with death.

Layer upon layer of skin falls away in patches,

and the deep red blood seeps quietly into

the sleepy portions of the earth.

On the Flyleaf of *The Master Letters*

We are not supposed to laugh when

we encounter someone disfigured,

unless we think they deserve holy

laughter, except we do not know

any of his or her descendants

belonged to a race of giants

who might be willing to rip out

our larynx or rip off an arm or

two because we displayed our

best improper manners.

A lesson in absolute courtesy.

Thus giants like our own mothers

think we should have had installed

in us proper courtesies before we

ventured into the world causing

intensive and severe harm.

On the Flyleaf of *Leaves of Hypnos*

Thick salve of youthful blood

balms the country's sores.

Still, it does not heal;

the ache is too great.

The pulse runs in halted breaths;

some are indistinguishably soft,

some are rougher than tree bark.

Trees begin to weep their leaves.

Water drenches the dry tubers,

those tender organs of wood

exposed to lice and vermin,

grey worms exiting dead bodies.

The river embraces the dead;

the dead cannot bury themselves.

The land loses all possibility

for sweet negotiations.

Breath uncovers the earth;

nothing is there.

The land returns to sand;

there are no prayers to be

found in the folds of clay.

The sun, the last

of the martyrs,

is dying.

On the Flyleaf of *Plenty*

In this London atmosphere
everyone here love, seems
as merry as any town is at
Christmastime, with their
mouths buried in cell phones,
like thin ostriches ignoring
all other heads in the sand
who are equally as busy
on phones which are tied
to other connections with
the following engaged signal:
Busy!
Busy!
Busy!

Invincibly determined, like those distant planets set in their predestined orbits, revolving, incessantly, and consistently around each other. Grafted on to each other like the steel of last breaths, demonstrating how acts should be done with small effective gestures. First, forbid all executions with wild iron tears black people used to exude at Baptists funerals. Time has made inquiry into how long the flesh can sustain forbearance. Still, physicians will only answer in vague terms: *Nothing is accurate.* Does he mean nothing as in: clocks, blenders, trash compactors, cars, lawn mowers, motor cycles, airplanes or simply the human heart? Perhaps he is still trying to *do no harm.* There will be no one to direct how to mourn the cold resplendency of life. Death is a reasoned passing. Take care to finalize all necessary details. Let surrounded friends recall the delicate stories of your life. Let all myths and legends be placed side by side in an undistinguished war of true and false. There is only so much one can do in arranging final details: watch a fire being extinguished, wait for a hurricane to subside, wait for the debris in a tornado to settle, then move into the clear silence and wait for another spring to approach.

On the Flyleaf of *The Lives of the Heart*

My mother knew after giving birth to me

that I would suffer enough needless pain,

which would not be of my own making,

so much so that she opted not to have me

circumcised. The world would do that

on its own. One less shock to my bodily

system may have been a part of her restive

thought, an inkling in the brain that this

one severe and early trauma could be

avoided because I would come to know

and question if it could have been

prevented, delayed? I suspect that there

could have been only one alternative,

and that is to have never been born.

On the Flyleaf of *Transformation*

In the assisted living facility
the attendant told me: *Your mother*
called for you all day long:
Hubbard? Hubbard?
When it was evening
she didn't call anymore.
She hasn't spoken since.
I think she has made her peace.
I think she can die now.
Was there no one who gave
a thought to call me? I am her
next of kin. She told me once
a similar story of her step-mother
on her dying bed calling for her,
but those who heard her knew the
misery she had caused and did not
call my mother, and so her
step-mother died unforgiven.
Why does her story haunt me
now that I know we are losing her?
I see her moving safely on.
Silence has a Sunday face.

On the Flyleaf of *Steal the Bacon*

In the forties

the houses in Birmingham were built of straw,

the landlords were thin niggardly slats,

the southern winters paid no attention,

those winds were the snarl of bare teeth

they could tear heart and self-respect apart.

Those men who were willing to collect the money

and interest from our fathers did not notice

the ramifications of what they took.

What could our fathers have done?

I know now that what I say is

in part the true history

of what happened. I know also that the

family lore is filled with work and alcohol.

Both stood to kill in those days.

Neither wife nor mother love

could stem the tide of such fatalities.

Lately, I have understood why my

uncles cried whiskey tears on Saturday nights,

and were too dizzy on Sunday mornings

to seek salvation. Their wives could

pray for that. That was their Sunday duty.

They were left to repair the work-week body

so they could be "ready to roll"

on Monday mornings,

and to do whatever was asked

of them by the boss man—

oblige his every requirement.

This is how we lived our lives

in the forties.

On the Flyleaf of *The Divided Country*

Believe in the catastrophe of love

the singeing poisonous whispers of love

the wrestle and pull

between pure and absolute.

The sun has its own natural violence

its suffocating radiance

falling in waves like dismembered butterfly wings

or interminable sounds of locust.

The leaves daily cut the air into thin silver banners—

Goldiva's modest hair, Medusa's brutal wisdom—

all they can before the onslaught of winter,

and the desperate wait for spring.

Something must renew the flesh;

something must invigorate the water;

something explode in the air;

something must trundle

the imagination.

On the Flyleaf of *Cold Comfort*

Oh Lord I just come the fountain, your name so sweet.

African American Spiritual

In Memory of Bessie Thomas, aged 112

I know why my father and his father before him and his father and all
the other fathers in this family never spoke to their sons about their
southern rearing. All the way back to the first boat which landed our
captured bodies on these shores with our sweet afflictions, we have
suppressed the initial shock and pain, determined to survive the irrational.
I will never recall such horrors of my southern upbringing for my
daughter either. Such struggles are unworthy inheritances. So quiet
has crept upon the unspoken order of the past centuries which I was so
unfortunately rattled into by the presence of my granddaughter who
asked: *Grandpa did you ever drink segregated water?* The
directness of such a question. I had to search for the miracle answer:
Yes, child. What makes you ask such a question?

I retold this story to a mature white woman who remembered she had
had a similar experience. She had asked her father: *Why can't I drink
from the colored fountain? Because,* he said: *those fountains contain
rainbow water. It is reserved for Negroes only. Well,* she recounted,
*from that moment on curiosity raged in my blood. I was determined
to drink some rainbow water or die. So one day when no one was
looking, I took a quick slow drink so that I could relish the taste of
all the colors. To my utter surprise that water contained no
miraculous colors. My disobedience confronted my father.* He smiled
and said: *Let that be significant to you. Rainbow water is the same
water we drink.*

On the Flyleaf of *Shadow Train*

    For: Larry Kensington

Pigeon dropping is like all excrement: human or animal. You have to recognize the menial difference. It is like viewing a Rembrandt or Sargent and arguing the palette of human difference. Still you will be reminded of the odor, the stench pressingly awful when one receives those urgent epistles begging:

Wondrous Dear Sir:

I am a secret executive working in The High and Mighty Bank of Zamu. We are located in the Province of The Third Principality which is as far away from Cairo as possible, under the last shifty sands of the Sahara Desert. I am the 29th son of King Mumbo Dumbo, recently deceased, and without his final will being probated. That is why I have had to take a job as a bank clerk in order to protect my rightful claims as one of my father's true heirs, as I continue to make ends meet for my family which I can barely afford to house and feed. My father had no daughters. So, all of my brothers are plotting against me with the mercenary colonels of the secret army. They have contrived to keep me from inheriting one ounce of gold from my father's wealth. Now without any political clout and as far away from ascending the throne as possible, I find myself in an unwitting position. I still have one secret which I alone am privy to. My father was a simple but wise man, no doubt suspected that there would be a plot against me; he warned me to be on my guard. He also informed me that there was a billion dollars in gold bullion and other valuables safely deposited in Switzerland under an assumed name which only I know. If you are willing to send me enough money to fly me and my wife and child to safety in Switzerland, I will happily share a fourth of my intended inheritance with you. You may act as an ambassador and representative of the late King and present yourself at the bank *and lay claim to the fortune that is held there. I need $25,000.00 in a cashiers check in order to make my escape from Zamu. My country has become a living prison for me and my family. I confide in you and tell you that I solicited your name from the very reputable United Trade Organization of Fools Anonymous which was founded by the American actor W. C. Fields. I know that you will not reject me or my cause. I simply venture to claim what is rightfully mine. I appeal to your American Democratic nature and willingness to help the down-trodden which as I understand it has always been the American Way! Please come to my rescue with a registered bank check in the amount of $25,000.00. For your investment in this venture, know, in the end, that you will become a very wealthy man. I look forward to hearing from you and having your reply in the next post. Let this be our secret. I remain your humble servant Prince Abo-Achoo Ka-Sneeze Shambuli, 29th heir to the late King Mumbo Dumbo in the Third Province in the Exhalted Principality of La La De De Uoop Bop Shebam in The Kingdom of Zamu.*

On the Flyleaf of *Small Congregations I*

When I remember Birmingham, Alabama, the forties was a time when

everything seemed absolutely acceptable, taken for granted although

the ordinary truth was nowhere to be found in my twelve-year-old eyes;

nothing in that town, in those claustrophobic days seemed oppressive.

The sun seemed content to come and go, as it pleased, without

impediment until the final shade of evening arrived and the humid

air settled or was moved occasionally by a woman positioned carefully

and comfortably in her front porch swing holding a church fan and

moving the evening air about as she pleases, to induce sleep.

Sometimes an old hymn could be heard as it surrounded her body

like a child being put to sleep, a rhythmic sedative applied,

a comfortable pallet prepared to soothe the wooden floors. Events

such as these were thought to be good; sometimes innocence knew

no better and was transformed while evening moved on to its own sleep.

On the Flyleaf of *Small Congregations* II

I remember the forties in Birmingham, Alabama when

it appeared absolutely acceptable, taken for granted and

although the ordinary truth was nowhere to be found in my

twelve years old eyes nothing in that town, resulting from

those claustrophobic days seemed oppressive.

The sun was content to come and go, as it pleased, without

impediment. The final shade of the afternoon arrived and

afterwards when the humidity settled, it was moved

occasionally by a woman positioned carefully, comfortably

on her front porch swing, holding a church fan and moving

the evening air gently about as she pleased, to induce slumber.

Sometimes an old hymn surrounded her body like a child

being tucked in, put to sleep, a rhythmic sedative applied,

a comfortable pallet prepared to soothe wooden floors.

Events such as these were thought to be good;

sometimes innocence knew no better and was transformed

while the evening moved on to its own sleep.

On the Flyleaf of *Musical Events*

Mostly when I shower these days

I am reminded of Carol Berge, not

lasciviously, but because she

demanded such clear and precisely

clean ligaments in each line of poetry

or prose meaning without dross,

absolute metaphor that strengthened

your walk without being didactic and

unpretentious. She knew the song of

a bird in the wild with a single breath

could herald the ease of night and day.

She was attentive to the skeleton,

the attachments which holds the bones

to muscles, and builds the architecture

of arteries and veins around said

structure so that all the melodies housed

in the body are safe. Now as the rinse

water floods my skin and drains effectively

away from my head, limbs, toes, legs

crotch, ankles and toes and are refreshed

in cleanliness and prepared, naturally,

to greet the perceptive world.

On the Flyleaf of *Selected Poems I*

These are the moments, the angular days the singular stress when love smiles and the dreams have been bitten by a ravenous snake gliding as hard as any wild horse, or the great bull of Orion trying to glimmer like stars but the light has become distant to the eye and helpless before rancid onions which still produces tears which begin to flow in righteous indignation like some promised river which kings, popes and common men have attempted to cross but hopelessly drown in failure. At such a moment we know we have lost an expensive life, while we are left to contemplate memory of money, of house and the unfortunate absence of love suddenly departed. Not the rub of cat, nor the whirr of factories working at full production, nor the table in the houses can produce enough bounty to get us sailing through another human day. I am reminded of her.

On the Flyleaf of *Stand Magazine* II

The morning windows wait for the first streaks of dawn

to slide through the split curtains and crawl across

the dusty wooden landing without ever sneezing or

waking my intrepid wife from her labor intensive sleep

because she thinks her body needs or desires another two

hours of beauty rest before she can begin the day, if,

indeed she is ever required or forced to accomplish a

stitch of work during her alert moments.

She must learn to face the quiet light and be enthralled

at the stillness that is in motion around her, and willingly

celebrate by witnessing the attending action.

It is abundantly clear like all knowledge that words were

here before form and shape and even substance were visible.

They did not take to the air utterly. This light like falcons,

and the lesser eagles soar only after first being urged or

reluctantly pushed from a place of safety before realizing

that they are one quarter of the space that they were once

suspicious of and now must learn to exhilarate in this air.

On the Flyleaf of *Roots and Branches*

When we buried you father, I purchased a copy of Robert Duncan's
Roots and Branches: images and sounds I thought destined to soothe
our grief and that cold Thanksgiving weekend when death summoned
you. When it was complete we dispersed and returned to our separate
griefs and private pleasures. You root and solidified branch, standing
solitary in the petrified wind. O tree, a hundred or more poems that
will spring forth as leaves: some darker, some greener than light,
other that will wither quickly to blinding dust, and some to a viral
darkness blind as shade or shadow. Gather the dead and lay them
in a quiet place.

On the Flyleaf of *Poems, Poets and Poetry*

These birds whether they be robins or sparrows
hop from venue to venue listening as it were for
those special sounds which are imminent beneath
the ground, and tells them that there are worms
tunneling back and forth moving towards some
unknown goal. Those birds have no visible
appendages that tell us birds can hear, so I am
guessing it is the motion of waves that tells them
where their next feast may be found. I have always
given wonder to why these birds move with their
heads cocked as if the wind is imparting some
unknown secret of exactly when the worn will
surface for air and come face to face with death.

On the Flyleaf of *Hunger*

I mailed a sand dollar to West Germany once;

it was white like a *femme fatale* with black

Hitchcock eyes. That dollar was part of the

western mystic, those late days of the

twentieth century. When the gift arrived

it was sand again. Despite cloth, cotton

and protective cardboard it was destined

to always be shifting sand, not art.

What could have survived that Atlantic

journey? It will come as no severe surprise

that sand, in spite of the pressures that

come to bear upon it, or shaken and sifted time

and time again, it will always retain its original

chemistry.

On the Flyleaf of *90 Miles*

For: Dennis Brutus

I see your restless spirit in between the roots of a Banyan tree
searching for a route that will allow you to defeat your nearest
competitor. Sound is the nuance which frees the body from
politics. You seek a clear path between the blades of light.
The sudden Hawaiian rains soothe the summer heat.
The wind is a breath of hindrance, an apartheid of clouds
hindering every citizen and placing them in prison because
they were wont to sing a song of resistance.

On the Flyleaf of *The Bluest Eye*

His mother swore on her private heart that
There never were any Insurance Men
sniffing around my front door and
hoping to slip out of her back door
unnoticed. I paid my bills on time;
I was never late. No company ever
had to garnishee my wages to
recoup their money. That was her
final declaration on the subject.
Even so, there remained an
indelible blue circle around
her son's eyes. A hole in the
ethereal blue, and there was
no one, given his mother's
sworn oath, to tell him otherwise.
The evidence says someone white
was lurking around his grandmother's
or great grandmother's kitchen,
like the black woman who held sway over
George Washington's barbeque pit
that she ultimately cooked her way
to freedom with a tad more barbeque
sauce than usual and ultimately
opened her own restaurant in New

York City. Now that is what I call cooking if your eyes have the slightest hint of blue in them.

On the Flyleaf of *Selected Poems* II

These are the moments, the angular days a singular time of stress

when love, the smiles and dreams have been bitten by a ravenous

rat scrambling as any wild horse to win a race, or the great bull of

Orion's fame trying to out glimmer all the stars, but the light has

faded, become distant before the hapless eye while visiting the

rancid onions which still produce tears of righteous indignation,

like the skin and bone survivors of the Holocaust, like some

promised river which kings, potentates and common men have

attempted to ford, but hopelessly drowned in failure. At such

moments we know we have lost the battle and are left to

contemplate the memory of house and family, money and the

unfortunate absence of love that suddenly departs. Not the rub

of cat, nor the whirr of factories working at full blast, nor the

calculations of production which failed to produce enough

bounty to get us sailing through another human day can save us.

On the Flyleaf of *These Days* I

The profound never occurs when you are looking.

It always happens when you least expect it to happen.

And sometimes the indivisible elements arrive absolutely

unseen like the ghost of some far away memory that

shakes a bird's egg from some high nesting branch.

It falls inexorably on the naked ground: it lies there until

I push my granddaughter past in her carriage, and see what

might have been a life lying there in the gutter. There will

be no descendent from this egg, no bird to lay claim to

whatever inheritance there might or will be. Reason does

not enter into our evening walk; logic is nowhere

to be engaged; it cannot be found. Circumstance

always lies camouflaged on the ground or hanging

just slightly out of reach in the air.

On the Flyleaf of *These Days* II

This tale begins in the afterglow of affection

when a sometimes significant entertainment

and an insignificant life merge like a sterling

force galvanizing the heart and taking all the

animals to the brink of belief in human good,

investing all its residual in the strength to

achieve unexpectedly ordinary goals. Keep

the feet in concert with the ground

while short-sighted vision watches the

whispers in wind. The smallest incendiaries

have been erased, one by one, taking no heed

of the failures that may occur in the blood,

the furious rage that could be etched on any

human brow. The self can be revived from

the damage of raging guns and forgiveness.

Memory and honor are the best clothes to

dress in.

On the Flyleaf of *Writing Poetry*

The old woman thinks King Lear:
his daughters, the prisons he suffered.
Although she is not royalty and does
not have nearly that much money or
property to dispense, still she must be
careful about disposing what she had
hoarded, a small. minute fortune.
Her life was based on independence.
Now all that is gone, faded into
memories with no way of recalling
a single event that occurred between
Tokyo and London, New York and
Chicago, and no way of ever
retrieving one cent of what she
might now affordably give away.

On the Flyleaf of *The Virgil*

Depending on the circumstances

never respond to an aggravated wife

hysterically as if you have been called

to execute some type of vermin or to

rescue a field mouse or wild bird from

the house cat's maw or attempt to

bandage a cracked wing or simply feed

some lost wretched animal. The ears

know how to respond quickly. It is

the stimuli of emergency that signals

surely when everything is finally over.

On the Flyleaf of *New and Selected Poems*

All physical activities but prayer
sit by my blood daughter's sick bed.
She trembles like a helicopter's wing
on a hospital heliport bringing a
severely injured person or
transporting organs packed in ice
desperate to maintain life. Surgeons,
physicians and nurses are called to
maintain the ordinary pulse of life.
In our human bodies we work farther
into old age than ever expected.
We thank these workers with
extraordinary hands who have their
own visions and do not yet know what
a terrible expenditure it is to repair
one single human heart.

On the Flyleaf of *No Other World*

A Southerner connects with the blue in my eyes;

he sees rings in my background and wonders

who put them there? I do not know.

My license states that my eyes are brown.

Who is to say where that blue came from

now that my mother and father are dead

and both sets of their parents are deceased?

Who is left to say what the history of this

blue implies? Somewhere in the deep dark

background someone white is languishing

there, waiting.

On the Flyleaf of *Fate*

Somewhere in the skin of the tightest drum

sealed in the soundless cement and buried

in the softest earth so that this block will

sink by its own accord further towards

the center of the earth where all is

boiling molten and no trace of life,

as we know it, is ever found.

There you are James Hoffa, unionist,

organizer, bare-fisted fighter waiting

for the opportunity to be hiccupped

upon the land you once knew and

walked as proudly as any man might,

creating endless enemies so that when

and if you return, to begin again

organizing the little man, and relying

on the effectiveness of your abilities,

you must take special care for those

enemies who ordered you be dispatched

and those who effectively carried out

those orders.

On the Flyleaf of *Atlantis*

Its name may be the weight of rain or something that allows the wind to push against the ribs from the inside: internal combustion. I know if I step out of the air I cannot go back. That step would be final, and as far as I can perceive there would only be a falling, a rushing explosion raking my face and unbuttoning my clothes, sucking my body down into pain and excruciating darkness. A bevy of voices of indeterminate chatter would be questioning: *Why? What made him do it? What did he think he would accomplish by this terrible and severe act?* When it was all over he would have to return to the beginning, start from scratch, make a better attempt at living or he would have to repeat the process again and again until he perfected it. That is why many of us pride ourselves on doing a thing right the first time around.

On the Flyleaf of *Angle of Ascent*

We are driving in Ohio North on I-75.
We are one hour away from our
destination, and have to stop to catch
our breath before we finally arrive,
visit, then retrace our way home again.
The road advises: *Keep Right!*
The shoulder ends in a quarter mile.
What is the meaning of shoulder's end?
Was this a Sunday morning drive,
a Sunday afternoon escape?
Only the wind knows
as it glazes the landscape.

On the Flyleaf of *My Mother's Body*

Poetry is a different kind of conversation.

I am standing in a purple olive grove;

I scratch my body against the earth of escape;

I am seeking a sweet space where I can breathe

sun, digest air, soak water, eat fire with my teeth

and tongue, smell a country I have never traveled.

I am an exile from slavery. There is darkness in

my bones. The holiness in my blood runs away.

Cold hounds are in pursuit of my leavings.

When they finally track me down, they will eat

of my muscled breast, through that opening

they will see a heart of testicles pulsing, holding

on to an electric freedom driven by hot footsteps,

fleeing the hooks of anger that could reel them in

like some marlin being reeled in all the way across

the middle passage to a land that would not love them.

On the Flyleaf of *The Gospel of Barbecue*

A mole, as blind as Milton who suffered earthly blindness,

has sought out the comfort of my back yard leaving mounds

of tunneled earth with thorough and infinitely undetectable

stealth. He plows beneath my manicured lawn until it resembles

the mountain range surrounding the Amazon River, carving out

a place for itself between sky and desert plains. I am forced

to confront this invincible critter. I want to destroy it with

spear and stones, but it hides underground, and will not show

itself, or allow me to exterminate it or take some ultimate

revenge upon it by placing its tiny body on our rotisserie.

On the Flyleaf of *Rough Music*

A young deer emerges from the deep woods,

gazes knowingly at the confusion my Mazda

makes at the edge of the road despite its age.

It knows it can kill and smash a windshield, crush

a fender or break a window and damage a door

with its bulk. Its eyes speak of total destruction

of that which is in its path which is impossible

to calculate. Those same eyes say: *Pass on by*

quickly, and it complies. The deer passes

behind me, vanishes into the darkness on

the other side.

On the Flyleaf of *Split Horizon*

A dusty white hawk

rises up through a

fierce morning mist

reaching towards

some damp outer

limit and as it does

it transforms itself

into a formidable

cloud, then glides

on into song.

On the Flyleaf of *From A Person Sitting In Darkness*

This house will be lonely, like death locked in its final coffin, when you are purposefully gone. Who knows or remembers what his or her mother said concerning those rivers which search for that final reservoir or how strong the forest trees are when rooting themselves slowly and deeper in the core of the earth and how they can hold a man weighing two hundred pounds or more by a single twisted thread until he can be found months later or the wind or sun or rain chooses to effectively release him from the bondage of his captivity because the fear that someone else might stumble upon his remains and have cause to die for similar offenses? Neither family nor friend had the courage to liberate a victim's body unless they did it in secret or was officially told to do so. Mothers always warned their sons to hold their spare and extravagant speech and to be frugal with their tongues, and to keep the tunnel of their throats closed good and tight until they could arrive as a quiet savior and arrange safe and lawful passage for them. Under such southern conditions one might be assured of life in spite of those indescribable horrors which beset Emmett Till. We are told witness is a house of goodness, and death is the threadbare presence of uncontrollable grief.

On the Flyleaf of *The Subterraneans II*

The wide horizon is filled with the courage of our footsteps,

the dawn has paused with its sure way of offering light,

the stone in the mountains will age with our footsteps,

the morning air precedes us as if it has the ability to light the way.

Our voices are gentle and not heavy like footsteps.

There are no arguments, here will be no dispelling of light.

On the Flyleaf of *Poems 1968-1999*

There is nothing mercenary about approaching

the apothecary for the proper pain medication

which will allow me to bury sanely without

an overwhelming fragrance of shit hanging

around embedded in the fabric of couch and

draperies. There is something about this dance

not even an emerging parlance, which is to

come afterwards when we are finished

moving forward. You deposit in front of me,

glances which, if I am correct, I should detect

a balance which tells me less and less about

the severe departure you will tout.

On the Flyleaf of *The Flashboat*

The husband/lover who is driving his wife/lover somewhere,

has a lecture of gestures built into his voice, arms and hands

which are not the thunderous and ignorant kind that will allow

her to damn whatever futile thoughts he may have entertained.

He will drive on until she screams stop and exits the vehicle

at some distant point at which time she will be able to execute

exactly what she had planned all along. She is, after all, her own

woman. She knows the rules of how to be a winner.

On the Flyleaf of *Hush* I

Light melancholy

somber wind

nothing spoken

flood of fire

lava distilled

nothing said

On the Flyleaf of *Hush* II

Sad light

furious wind

cold fire

tepid wind

no sound

no speech

On the Flyleaf of *Atlantis* I

A Yellow Jacket skirts the dangerous rim of a cup of hot tea.
He, no doubt, is aware of his hypnotic reflection, and like
Narcissus before him falls in love with his hopeless image.
He does not recognize his face; he is intrigued beyond
ordinary investigation. The steam of water anticipates a
dizzying and untimely death, a casting off of skin and tea.
It is the image that invites one toward the havoc of a kiss,
and no matter how blissful the embrace, death ends in
paradise. A similar death has occurred with a Humming Bird
feeder, when no hand was able to reach the excess of this
accidental fatality. So the body of one bee floats as if it were
preserved in amber. The yellow and black dazzles in sweetened
formaldehyde, although I am told that pure water will begin the
arduous task of peeling away the body, layer by layer, as if it were
an onion ready to reveal its marvelous inner secret of making tears.

On the Flyleaf of *Brutus' Orchard*

An anonymous man peers through random windows.
He is not a poet or singer, artist, musician nor
industrialist. He looks for inspiration because that is
what he thinks women are. I have not spoken to him
directly; I have only seen him commit the act.
Nothing should be discounted should he be found
suddenly dead. I have deemed his intrusive looks
should be rewarded with scalding water heated
on the gas burner. His screams should alert the night.
They should stab my neighbors who are involved
with their own nightly occupations. They will
ignore such impending warnings, realizing only
for the moment that they truly love each other.
Each night afterwards the man will return with
his aching scars. He is blind in one eye; he seeks
to discover if there is a new and terrible punishment
for the one eye left? I should tell you, I am a
descendent of the dreaded Borgias. I am in
possession of the family poisons more deadly
than speech. I am prepared for his voyeuristic
visits; still I will grant him no special liberties.
Tonight when he arrives, I will be waiting outside,
positioned behind the green holly shrubs.
When he focuses his good eye toward the bedroom

window, I shall punish him with the holly thorns.
I have painted them with a vitriolic poison that
will begin to eat slowly at the base of his cornea
and then move toward his spine. He will suffer
a paralysis of flesh, then his thoughts; he will
forget to relish the beautiful and only pay
attention to the roughly hewn. I will keep him
now fully debilitated in the cold family vault.

On the Flyleaf of *Firekeeper*

Before anything else was created
in the world, there was this tubular
snake that crawled through the
womb of the earth, thick as an
adult arm, all sun yellow with
black macadam lines shading the
center of its gossamer skin.
Then came the grouses, who,
having successfully mated were
left like attached Siamese twins
to their families foraging for
the necessary food, under the eyes
of suspicious spectators: from birds
to mushrooms exploding beneath
the feet, to the mammoth sharks
and whales whose teeth have
become the rough neglected sand
waiting to devour something smaller,
defenseless and less clever. The waters
of such animals weigh in on me with
their heavy beauty.

On the Flyleaf of *Everyday and Prophetic*

Curiosity watches the evening shadows descend like silk,

a velvety dark enclosure of worries

which is always in front of what can be seen clearly

when the hand reaches

for the softness of skin and the fullness of gentle lips.

The oldest son enters a constructed privacy,

flooded with severe light and invasive eyes.

The thought of protective darkness dissipates;

it will be a long time before his sensuous self

awakens to this possibility.

On the Flyleaf of *The Errancy*

In my seventieth year, cicadas
bore up through the solid earth,
after so many sleep-filled years;
it was a resurrection of small
insects taking place as an event
and with my cousin dying as another.
I didn't cry;
terrible distance had removed
all my tears, sucked the ducts dry
into the atmosphere where seemingly
all rain gathers to shower the living
and the dead, all at once from
indiscrete clouds interminably
engaged in refreshing song.
I did not attend his funeral;
I sent roses instead.
He and blood relatives before him
and the numerous ones who will
come after us have begun the
simplest of journeys, knowing
how to aid one another.
We, who survive, are left behind
to make new adjustments.
Dying is serious business.

On the Flyleaf of *The Man of Letters*

I push the heart

when snow falls lightly;

I thrust the heart

when water causes fright;

I embrace the heart

in the descending night;

I shush the heart

when other things remain quiet;

I urge the heart

when no one else will speak;

I shelter the heart

when floor boards squeak;

I encourage the heart

when gentle walls creak;

I push the heart

when the arctic walks;

I listen to the heart

when tree-bark talks.

On the Flyleaf of *Rain*

Everyday an Iraqi causes the bodies of his countrymen
to be shredded like parade confetti and rained down
upon the land he claims to love. There is no substance
to be taken from the land after such a drenching.
The air takes the blood and turns it into unleavened
bread. Only the stench of breath languishes; no love is
lost here, no freedom won. I have lost faith in the
morning cartoon's ability to rebound, to be full of life
after being crushed by impossible odds, nor do they
save the world as they do on television each and every
morning while the children of the world ready themselves
for school and the possibility of learning something entirely new.

On the Flyleaf of *Thieves of Paradise*

Mozart practiced with the diligence

of the worker ant who seems to hoard

all that it can carry, like Sisyphus bound

inexorably to that fierce cargo until

some minor god allowed him to

intermittently breathe between

carrying that rock and setting it down:

the requirement of fast ascending

arpeggios and those quietly descending

crescendos which mark the best musicians

who are given the brilliant but tormented

risk of making music.

On the Flyleaf of *Homage To Mistress Bradstreet*

The ships, birth-like coffins ceremoniously

sailing from indelible port to indelible port,

writing down invisible history between the

waves and the land and leaving it all for

some future generation to discover as they

try effectively to import life and death and

other unknown atrocities across that which

will be named a natural sea. The bones of

fish will remain as translucent as our ancestor's

history and as sharp as death; no lessons to be

taken from those waters; nothing redeeming

to be found even in a dead gesture riding

upon the natural waves.

On the Flyleaf of *Atlantis* II

The weight of rain thunders against his ribs

his lightening steps electrify the air

everything rushes

plummeting through space

Icarus's excruciating pain

questioning the dark

about purpose and accomplishment

asking forgiveness of the radical cold

for invoking fire as a present

as a proper gesture

On the Flyleaf of *Looking For Luck*

Razor thin snow

fell on our town

last night and cut

a severe path though

its breaths, altering

everything but

silence.

On the Flyleaf of *In Mad Love and War*

You Mr. Mahmoud Ahmaddinejad are
a sharp needle stabbing America's eye.
Who among us will wince knowing
something is wrong, no matter who
commits the act. You seem to be
digging for something deeper,
something commercially blind.
If you are bitten by a snake and
left untreated, what need is there
for more poison? Some individuals
are always on guard; some will never
surrender that flesh which would declare you
victor. In the third and fourth decades of
the Second World War there were heinous
acts we closed our eyes to. We will never be
deceived again, never forget; we will keep our
eyes open to what your hands are capable of, keep
our gaze focused, cautious about deception and the
spread of venom. You are an extraordinary weaver of
stories, some citizens will become addicted to your tales.
There is a dance to your words, a warmth that is enveloping,
seductive that perceives how readily you violate the
constitution of flesh.

On the Flyleaf of *The Last Lecture*

In a fluted pot of pink flowers,
a wren settles in to nurture the
three freshly lain eggs.
It recognizes my magpie eyes
invading the wonder of safety
in its nesting place and at once
abandons these finely crafted eggs,
leaves them to the wild wind, rain,
and other predators like snakes or
squirrels and whatever can reach that high
and spacious place whose memories are
built on mere chance and coincidence
like burying persimmons and acorns
in the same nest with abandoned eggs and
thereby crushing all expectations of birth.

On the Flyleaf of *Blessing the Boat*

Do I tell my daughter that her particular
chosen lover's sperm will be a viral infection
in her body, that she will be allergic always to
his known passions and that they alone will
someday make her life a prison unto itself?

On the Flyleaf of *Poetry: A Pocket Anthology*

The clouds spit.

The air crackles with electricity.

A dark mist of uncertainty cloaks the land.

A hawk's shadow radiates on the ground.

The weight of its presence plows through the humidity.

Something takes hold of a dark feather and allows it to

float carelessly through the open space writing it name fiercely.

On the Flyleaf of *The Voice of the Poet*

Mother did all the family laundry.
She was privy to the brief physical
stains which spoke to her son's wild
feminine attractions. She saw the tell-tale
signs that did not lie, nor create a false
impression. Mother used bleach to wash
and rinse away the sweat of incriminating evidence.
She sent it all down the drain of forgetful concern
before it could display pride or revelation
in an existence of its own.

On the Flyleaf of *April Galleons* II

Terror assaults a Russian school yard where
grief is the song of the mothers passing by.
A black mother, a continent away, observes:
Our children are supposed to bury us.
Consensus expects us to lay them in the earth,
Blood will thunder in our ears.
Sometimes words drown powerful men.
Skeletons of thought cannot be trusted.
The mothers gather up their dignity
along with their reserves; they strut
carefully ahead, their bodies erect
eyes forward, watching the stones
casually thrown by wind or citizen.
They observe a televised bier which
contains a body that once was promise;
now it is all faulty grief.

On the Flyleaf of *50 Contemporary Poets*

Beginning with a line from an older poet:
each generation tells the next how excellent
its time was and that the next generation will
have it better. That is the way tradition is born,

ritual begun. They will have it better just as I have

had it better than my father's century, and he must

have prevailed over his father's time. My daughter,

who is a lawyer, will do better than all of her ancestors

because she knows the law and how to circumvent its twists

and paradoxes and she knows how to bend it to her will.

On the Flyleaf of *Selected Letters* I

I search for all the possibilities for the world
and am happy that I am a part of the process
like the distant Tibetan who becomes a mystic
and fashions gods out of clay: air, fire, water,
words, jade, and lime stone. An absolute point
of ease is achieved since all things are richly made
or born. Assemble all your efforts between cough and
sneeze. The ground is my domain, the Taj Mahal
stands in alabaster shade. The Brooklyn Bridge
squeezes the wind making harp like songs as it flows
through its strings. I am confident of both joy and
pain; they come and go and will again and again
between light and shade between cough and sneeze.

On the Flyleaf of *To the Lighthouse*

Because we need so desperately to go
towards the lighthouse of our being,
I offer hope for you and me, along with
the saving grace of the light which
conducts and guides the sea, safely
inward to all harbors. As light escapes
through filtered windows, let us try to
escape into words and the nuances
that words engender. We know that time
still passes through everything, even
windows and is the same beam which
windows and is the same beam which
brings us back time and time again to
the lighthouse.

On the Flyleaf of *Alliance, Illinois*

Husband and wife in tandem,

in a bed, in a kitchen celebrating

a natural pleasure that grows in

pathological dirt. They ultimately

wash themselves with the available

light that beams into their bathroom

through an observant ceiling window

thinking all the while that the dust

like riff-raff debris that comes and

goes inside and out without luminosity

or consequence.

On the Flyleaf of *The Subterraneans* III

In Birmingham,

in the forties, the old women swept

their front porches first, then swept

the yard of unnecessary debris.

They must have felt they had to keep

everything clean, even though they did

not possess the accurate implements

to work with, their cleaning was executed

with the fervor of the religious, and the prayer

and song of the devout. In this way they kept

the dignity of their neighborhoods stable and radiant.

On the Flyleaf of *50 Contemporary Poets* II

With each generation, one half argues
that the world is all about money, and the
remaining half thinks that it is not about
money. I find myself on the fence of this
debate. I am squarely in the middle because
it is about money and intellect and social
mobility and arm in arm status. It is a unified
way of perceiving life. So it is, in the end, all
about money and purchasing the life you
think you deserve.

On the Flyleaf of *Collected Poems*

The house is demolished now.
A parking lot occupies the space.
The second floor has vanished into
thin air where once I had a delusion
that my soul floated outside my body
and paused to watch if I would recover
somehow from the fevers which ravaged
my flesh. Observing my predicament, like
a newly minted on-call physician my spirit
rejoined my flesh and promised never to
depart again. Such was the sensation that day
that it left me wondering who would believe
me if I told them what had taken place?

On the Flyleaf of *The Blacker The Berry*

For: Edith

Who, white as she was, always kept

her eyes on the prize of fairness.

White woman, now eighty,

came for a cool drink of water

before she died. She found she

was not welcome to sit at the

counter with her black friends,

nor was she allowed to register

her colored neighbors to vote.

A hurricane of memories floods

her skin as she watches four

decades of her own celluloid

history. Once she had the agility

of a gazelle, the quickness of

a minute. Now, her calcified

bones restrict her, She no

longer leaps , but now she

projects her flourishing

tears towards some earthly

good.

On the Flyleaf of *The Past*

Obstinate tears

utterances granted

a woman in blue stockings

my tongue is fragmented

an open wound

ears are there

haughtily dumb

to those tears

begging

the human heart

that grows dumb

in a glazed night

where the wind is a bitter eraser

the ears are dumber still

a neighbor watches

the decline of the human heart.

On the Flyleaf of *This Body Is Made of Camphor and Gopherwood*

Scrub the bath tub
and the kitchen floor
vacuum the rugs
open the back door

clean the windows
make the bed
hang the curtains
lie down, play dead

set the dining room table
insert the extra leaves
iron the table cloth
invite two thieves

read a book drive a Porche
write some song lyrics
sing the song
make it daring

steep some tea
add some milk
stir it smooth
as silk; walk the

dog; clear the attic

stay where you are.

On the Flyleaf of *Poems 1965-1975*

(a non Spenserian sonnet)

When they were not drinking, the family men:

my father, David, along with my uncles: Addison,

Peter, and Bud who ventured into righteous sin

in Birmingham from country, city on a dare.

They would disappear. Where they went,

I do not know. They returned with affection

in the evenings with a few measly dollars lent

or borrowed which they promptly contributed

to our necessary larder, the need for: flour, meal,

sugar black-eyed peas, salt pork and greens

delectable greens. They accompanied their

frightening tasks repetitively day in and out

leaving me to question who would teach me

the technical mysteries of exactly what they did,

when they vanished during those long days

when I was seven years old and had no

marketable skills to speak of?

On the Flyleaf of *Crow*

When the middle of the war-torn forties

came apart at the Southern seams, like

those Jewish families, interned in German

camps, who were gassed into oblivion,

incinerated into dust so that no human presence

was left to be detected, no DNA left to be discovered,

not even the slightest flake, one might think, could have

survived, you were living in another country and would

never cross paths or have anniversaries but became a

night owl, a tomcat on the prowl for loose experiences,

never wary of losing your subway dime or the time it took

to locate one promising experience. The slot machine criminally

takes away money that does not belong to it and refuses to reward

you with the simplest pack of Juicy Fruit.

On the Flyleaf of *Carnival Evening*

November 22, 1963,
I know exactly where I was,
having hitch-hiked a ride home
from the university.
I was visiting Harriet G.
In hindsight her husband Leo would die
the next year having unsuccessfully battled cancer.
She would follow him a year later after securing an
adoptive home for their only daughter.
The national news that afternoon introduced us to
prayer and reflection, it left us breathless and naked.
I went home to find prayer, to bend my knees
to the wooden floor, to weep fearfully, to turn on the
television and watch quietly while my heart pounded
senselessly, even though all the doors were locked and
no one could get in. Four years later
my mother's voice greeted me
as I came down the stairs for morning coffee.
Someone has shot Bobby Kennedy.

On the Flyleaf of *Absolute Trust in the Goodness of the Earth*

The old man tells the radical story of the longitude of his lawn.

The grass he says, *is in complete and total revolt.*

I have not mowed my back yard in two weeks.

A corp of weeds has instituted a coup d'etat from North to South.

Every white and purple gladiola has been sentenced to decapitation.

Nothing blooming is to be left alive or standing.

The horde of avenging green will institute a new order

before the remaining roses called Mr. Lincoln,

that revolutionary rose of Springfield awakens

his red to bleed on the diminishing winter snow

while the other roses, white and yellow burst and

bloom in the defiant sun. The astonishing grass

must be trimmed and manicured while other areas

remain hostile for the protection of animals and birds

to come and go, like the three nestlings whose blue eggs

fascinated my youngest granddaughter and now they lie

shattered, while the young have been fed and fattened,

and finally flown away without forwarding communications,

and this descendant has a flood of regret not seeing their first

flight. She will come to terms, in some later years, having

learned that animal, bird and humans intentionally seek a way

to travel effectively on their own. This is all the mysterious news

I have from the latitude of the home front, said the old man.

On the Flyleaf of *Opened Ground*

A Persian house cat stalks the garden
(while a deep dark silence envelopes
the surrounding green and settled foliage)
seeking the inevitable but waning sunlight.
The cat moves it hesitant muscles quietly.
Small birds suddenly slice the late air
singing guttural warnings about
impending death by sharp claw and fang,
instruments that puncture neck and heart
without warning, pursuing the core of the
pulse which signals the body's desire to
survive. Birds are always singing to the
unawares to take the secure air or disappear
into a safe and relative darkness like those
American slaves who could no longer willingly
endure whip or branding iron for their personal
rebellion. So they slipped inevitably into a scullery
black where neither skin nor hair was ever seen again.

On the Flyleaf of *The Last Uncle*

I open *The Last Uncle* on a page using an envelope as a book mark;
I read the "43rd Anniversary" poem by Linda Pastan. You may
never have read her, but it becomes abundantly clear by the expert
placement of her words that she is patently aware of you and that you
are in her imagination. She is an intuitive magician, who understands the
clever blocking of a play better than directors and knows by instinct the
glory of how one art intersects with all the other arts.

On the Flyleaf of *Urania*

titanic language.

clouds forget: they drift away.

sweet delirium.

Herbert Woodward Martin was Professor of English and Poet-In-Residence at The University of Dayton for more than three decades where he taught Creative Writings and African American Literature. He is the author of eight previous volumes of poetry. He has devoted an equal number of decades to editing and giving performances of the works of the Dayton poet and novelist Paul Laurence Dunbar. For his scholarly work Martin has been awarded four Honorary Doctor of Humane Letters. Martin is noted for his wide range of interests in music and art. He has closely collaborated with a number of American composers among whom are: Joseph Fennimore, Adolphus Hailstork and Philip Carl Magnuson. He has written the texts and librettos for two operas, one cantata and one Magnificat. A significant number of his poems have been set to music as well. He is the recipient of The Ohio Governor's Award. Most recently Martin has found himself a narrator for a number of symphonic works including a new recording of William Grant Still's *Symphony #1 The Afro-American* with The Dayton Philharmonic Symphony as well as Aaron Copland's *Lincoln Portrait*.

Sources by Title and Author

Absolute Trust in the Goodness of the Earth	Alice Walker
Alliance, Illinois	Dave Etter
Angle of Ascent	Robert Hayden
The Answers Are Inside the Mountains	William Stafford
April Galleons	John Ashbery
Atlantis	Mark Doty
Autobiographies	Alfred Corn
Blacker the Berry	Wallace Thurman
The Bluest Eye	Toni Morrison
Blessing the Boats	Lucille Clifton
The Book of Light	Lucille Clifton
Brutus's Orchard	Roy Fuller
By the Light of My Father's Smile	Alice Walker
Carnival Evenings	Linda Pastan
Cold Comfort	Wanda Coleman
Collected Poems	James Wright
Crow	Ted Hughes
The Errancy	Jorie Graham
Everyday and Prophetic	Nick Halpern
Fate	Ai
Firekeeper	Patti Ann Rodgers
The Flashpoint	Jane Cooper
50 Contemporary Poets	Alberta Turner
From A Person Sitting In Darkness	Gerald Barrax
The Gospel of Barbeque	Honoree Fanonne Jeffers
Homage To Mistress Bradstreet	John Berryman
Hunger	Lucie Brock-Broido
Hush	David St. John
In Mad Love and War	Joy Harjo
The Invention of The Zero	Richard Kenney
The Last Lecture	Randy Pausch
The Last Uncle	Linda Pastan
Leaves of Hypnos	Rene Char
The Lives of The Heart	Jane Hirshfield
Looking For Luck	Maxine Kumin

BOTTOM DOG PRESS
BOOKS IN THE HARMONY SERIES

On the Flyleaf: Poems
By Herbert Woodward Martin, 104 pgs. $16
The Stolen Child: A Novel
By Suzanne Kelly, 350 pgs. $18
The Canary: A Novel
By Michael Loyd Gray, 192 pgs. $18
The Harmonist at Nightfall: Poems of Indiana
By Shari Wagner, 114 pgs. $16
Painting Bridges: A Novel
By Patricia Averbach, 234 pgs. $18
Ariadne & Other Poems
By Ingrid Swanberg, 120 pgs. $16
The Search for the Reason Why: New and Selected Poems
By Tom Kryss, 192 pgs. $16
Kenneth Patchen: Rebel Poet in America
By Larry Smith, Revised 2nd Edition, 326 pgs. Cloth $28
Selected Correspondence of Kenneth Patchen,
Edited with introduction by Allen Frost,
312 pgs. Paper $18/ Cloth $28
Awash with Roses: Collected Love Poems of Kenneth Patchen
Eds. Laura Smith and Larry Smith
With introduction by Larry Smith, 200 pgs. $16

* * * *

HARMONY COLLECTIONS AND ANTHOLOGIES
d.a.levy and the mimeograph revolution
Eds. Ingrid Swanberg and Larry Smith, 276 pgs. $20
Come Together: Imagine Peace
Eds. Ann Smith, Larry Smith, Philip Metres, 204 pgs. $16
Evensong: Contemporary American Poets on Spirituality
Eds. Gerry LaFemina and Chad Prevost, 240 pgs. $16
America Zen: A Gathering of Poets
Eds. Ray McNiece and Larry Smith, 224 pgs. $16
Family Matters: Poems of Our Families
Eds. Ann Smith and Larry Smith, 232 pgs. $16

Bottom Dog Press, Inc.
PO Box 425/ Huron, Ohio 44839
Order Online at:
http://smithdocs.net

CPSIA information can be obtained at www.ICGtesting.com
Printed in the USA
LVOW05s1449081213

364376LV00003B/127/P